LEGENDARY FOOTBALL STORIES

Fun & Inspirational Facts & Stories of the Greatest Football Players and Games of All Time

---

FALCON FOCUS

Copyright © 2023 Falcon Focus

All rights reserved. No part of this publication may be reproduced, distributed or transmitted in any form or by any means, including photocopying, recording, or other electronic or mechanical methods, without the prior written permission of the publisher, except in the case of brief quotations embodied in critical reviews and certain other non-commercial uses permitted by copyright law.

Trademarked names appear throughout this book. Rather than use a trademark symbol with every occurrence of a trademarked name, names are used in an editorial fashion, with no intention of infringement of the respective owner's trademark. The information in this book is distributed on an "as is" basis, without warranty. Although every precaution has been taken in the preparation of this work, neither the author nor the publisher shall have any liability to any person or entity with respect to any loss or damage caused or alleged to be caused directly or indirectly by the information contained in this book.

American football is more than a game; it's a saga played out on a field of green. Every snap is a story, every tackle a triumph, and every pass a piece of art painted in the air. In this arena, every touchdown is a tale of teamwork, every field goal a feat of precision, and every play a dance of strategy and strength. On this gridiron, legends are born, resilience is tested, and every yard gained is a step toward glory etched in the memories of both players and spectators.

Contents

Introduction	v
1. Walter Payton's Grace	1
2. Peyton Manning's Comeback	11
3. The Immaculate Reception	22
4. Sarah Fuller's Historic Kick	32
5. The Ice Bowl	42
6. Derrick Coleman's Inspiring Journey	53
7. The Legend of Jerry Rice	63
8. The Iron Will of Brett Favre	73
9. The Revolutionary Tony Dungy	84
References	95
Bonus: Free Book!	97

Introduction

Welcome, football aficionados, to a realm filled with the awe, challenges, and unforgettable experiences of football! *Legendary Football Stories* is a voyage into the soul of the sport, uncovering the dedication, resilience, and spirit that shape some of football's most extraordinary characters.

Dive into these pages to discover the elegance of Walter Payton, whose grace extended both on and off the field, and experience Peyton Manning's remarkable comeback, a testament to resilience and dedication. Witness the magical Immaculate Reception, a symbol of hope and luck that forever changed NFL history, and draw inspiration from Sarah Fuller's historic kick, breaking gender barriers and redefining what's possible in sports.

Feel the icy chill of the legendary Ice Bowl, a story of mental and physical fortitude under extreme conditions, and be moved by Derrick Coleman's inspiring journey, overcoming deafness to reach the NFL's pinnacle. Marvel at Jerry Rice's legendary career, where hard work and dedication set new standards for wide receivers, and delve into the iron will of Brett Favre, whose resilience and grit defined his storied career.

Finally, explore the revolutionary impact of Tony Dungy, a coach who broke racial barriers and left a legacy beyond the field, emphasizing integrity, leadership, and community involvement.

Each story in this collection extends beyond mere gameplay, revealing the human elements of football – the triumphs, the adversities, and the steadfast spirit of those who cherish the game. Whether you're a budding player, a devoted fan, or a lover of stirring tales, these narratives are for you. So, strap on your helmet, get ready to cheer, and embark on a journey that captures the essence of football and the life lessons it imparts. Join us as we explore the magic and inspiration football brings to people worldwide!

Walter Payton's Grace

Biography

Walter Payton, affectionately known as "Sweetness" for his graceful playing style and exceptional character, is a revered figure in the history of the NFL. Born on July 25, 1954, in Columbia, Mississippi, Walter Payton's journey in football began in his high school years. Despite facing initial setbacks, including being left off the high school varsity team in his sophomore year, Payton's resilience and natural talent quickly came to the forefront. By the time he was a senior, he had become a standout player, known for his speed, agility, and tenacity.

Payton's college career at Jackson State University further solidified his status as a formidable athlete. He excelled in the university's football program, amassing a series of impressive records and accolades. His time at Jackson State was marked not only by his athletic prowess but also by his academic diligence, illustrating his commitment to excellence in all facets of life.

In 1975, Walter Payton's entry into the NFL marked the beginning of what would be an extraordinary professional career. He was selected in the first round, fourth overall, by the Chicago Bears in the NFL Draft. This transition to the professional league was a significant step for Payton, who brought with him not only his athletic abilities but also a work ethic and a level of professionalism that would become his hallmarks.

From the outset of his NFL career, Payton demonstrated a unique combination of power, agility, and grace. His running style, characterized by an uncanny ability to avoid tackles and break long runs, quickly made him one of the most exciting players to watch in the league. Payton wasn't just a runner; he was also a skilled receiver and a willing blocker, making him an all-around asset to the Bears' offense.

Beyond his physical talents, Payton was known for his humility and grace. He approached the game with a respect and love that endeared him to fans and fellow players alike. His sportsmanship and dedication to the sport were evident in every game he played, making him not just a great player but also a great ambassador for football.

Career Highlights

Walter Payton's NFL career, spanning from 1975 to 1987 with the Chicago Bears, is marked by a multitude of achievements and a playing style that left an indelible mark on the sport. Known for his incredible endurance, versatility, and the poetic grace with which he played, Payton's career highlights are a testament to his status as one of the greatest running backs in NFL history.

Payton's playing style was a unique blend of agility, power, and finesse. He had an extraordinary ability to evade tackles with his elusive moves, often leaving defenders grasping at air. Payton wasn't just agile; he was also known for his remarkable strength and toughness, consistently breaking tackles and gaining extra yards through sheer willpower and effort. His endurance was legendary, as he rarely missed games and seemed to get stronger as the game progressed, embodying the workhorse running back archetype.

One of Payton's most notable career achievements was becoming the NFL's all-time leading rusher, a record he held at the time of his retirement. He amassed 16,726 rushing yards over his illustrious career, a testament to his durability and consistency. Payton also scored 110 rushing touchdowns, showcasing his effectiveness in the red zone and his role as a key player in the Bears' offense.

Payton's single-game performance on November 20, 1977, against the Minnesota Vikings was one for the ages. He rushed for an astounding 275 yards, setting an NFL record for most rushing yards in a single game, a record that stood for 23 years. This performance exemplified Payton's extraordinary talent and his ability to dominate games.

In 1977, Payton was honored as the NFL's Most Valuable Player (MVP), recognizing his contributions to the Bears and his excellence on the field. His MVP season was marked by incredible performances and leadership, further cementing his reputation as one of the league's top players.

Payton's career wasn't just about individual statistics; he was a crucial member of the 1985 Chicago Bears team that won Super Bowl XX. This victory was a crowning achievement in his career, giving him a well-deserved championship ring. Payton's contributions to the team's success were invaluable, although he was famously not given the opportunity to score a touchdown in the Super Bowl, a decision that head coach Mike Ditka later regretted.

Beyond his on-field achievements, Payton was known for his exemplary character and sportsmanship. He played the game with a level of respect and joy that endeared him to both teammates and opponents. His commitment to excellence, both on and off the field, left a lasting legacy in the NFL.

Off-field Activities and Humanitarian Work

Walter Payton's impact extended well beyond the football field, with his off-field activities and humanitarian work underscoring his commitment to making a positive difference in the lives of others. His contributions outside of football were marked by the same grace and dedication that he exhibited as a player, making him not only a legend on the field but also a respected and beloved figure in the community.

Payton's philanthropic efforts were varied and impactful. He was deeply involved in numerous charitable activities, focusing particularly on helping children and young people. One of his notable contributions was the establishment of the Walter Payton Foundation, which aimed to provide assistance and support to underprivileged children. The foundation's work included educational programs, scholarship funds, and numerous initiatives designed to uplift and empower youth.

In addition to his foundation, Payton was known for his personal involvement in charitable causes. He frequently made appearances at schools, hospitals, and community events, where he interacted with fans and community members. His visits, especially to children's hospitals, were marked by a genuine desire to bring joy and hope to those he met. Payton's warmth and kindness in these interactions left a lasting impression on those he encountered.

Payton also played a significant role in promoting organ donation. After being diagnosed with a rare liver disease in the late 1990s, he became an advocate for organ transplants and donor awareness. His openness about his condition and his efforts to raise awareness about the importance of organ donation brought national attention to the cause, potentially saving many lives.

Moreover, Payton's commitment to community and humanitarian work extended to mentoring young athletes and supporting fellow football players. He often shared his experiences and insights, helping guide the next generation of players both on and off the field. His mentorship was driven by a belief in the importance of character, discipline, and giving back, values that he consistently embodied.

Personality and Character

Payton's humility was one of his most defining traits. Despite his superstar status and numerous accolades, he remained grounded and approachable. He never sought the spotlight for personal glory but rather focused on the success of his team and the joy of playing the game. This humility endeared him to teammates, coaches, and fans alike, as he consistently deflected praise onto others and emphasized the collective effort over individual achievements.

His work ethic was legendary. Payton's commitment to excellence was evident in his rigorous training regimen and his relentless pursuit of improvement. He was known for his intense off-season workouts, which included running steep hills and extensive strength training. This dedication to conditioning not only made him one of the most durable and effective players in the NFL but also set a standard for future generations of athletes. Payton's approach to practice and preparation demonstrated his belief that talent alone was not enough; success required hard work and perseverance.

Respect for others was a cornerstone of Payton's character. He treated everyone, from teammates and coaches to fans and opponents, with kindness and consideration. His sportsmanship on the field was exemplary; he played the game with intensity but always within the bounds of fairness and respect for the competition. Off the field, Payton's interactions were marked by a genuine interest in others and a willingness to listen and engage. He valued the relationships he built throughout his life, whether in the context of football or in his broader community interactions.

Additionally, Payton's character was marked by a sense of joy and love for life. He approached both football and his off-field activities with a zest and enthusiasm that was infectious. His positive attitude, even in the face of personal and professional challenges, was a testament to his strength of character and his ability to inspire and uplift those around him.

Legacy

As a player, Payton is etched in the annals of NFL history as one of the greatest running backs ever. His record-breaking career, marked by an unmatched combination of agility, power, and endurance, set new standards for future generations of running backs. Payton's name is synonymous with greatness in football, and his playing style—characterized by its grace, tenacity, and flair—left an indelible impression on both fans and fellow players. His legacy in the sport is further immortalized by the NFL's Walter Payton Man of the Year Award, given annually to a player who exemplifies excellence on and off the field.

Beyond his athletic prowess, Payton's legacy as a person is equally significant. He is remembered for his humility, kindness, and commitment to making a positive impact in the lives of others. His philanthropic endeavors, particularly those aimed at helping children and advocating for organ donation, showcased his compassion and selflessness. Payton's approach to life, characterized by a relentless work ethic and a profound respect for others, made him a role model not just for athletes, but for people from all walks of life.

Payton's personality also left a lasting impact. His joyfulness, resilience in facing adversity, and the genuine love he had for football and life itself continue to inspire many. He approached challenges, both on and off the field, with a positive attitude and a determination to succeed, qualities that endeared him to many and contributed to his enduring legacy.

Moreover, Payton's legacy is seen in the way he influenced the culture of football and sportsmanship. He played the game with a level of integrity and honor that set a high bar for how athletes should conduct themselves in competition. His legacy continues to influence the attitudes and behaviors of players at all levels of the sport.

Life Lessons

The life of Walter Payton, marked by extraordinary grace both on and off the field, offers a wealth of lessons for individuals, providing valuable guidance on character, perseverance, and the true meaning of success.

One of the primary lessons from Payton's life is the importance of hard work and dedication. His incredible work ethic, both in training and during games, demonstrated that achieving greatness requires consistent effort and commitment.

Payton's humility, despite his immense success, is another powerful lesson. He showed that true greatness is accompanied by modesty and a willingness to share success with others. This humility, evident in the way he interacted with teammates, fans, and the community, teaches the value of remaining grounded and grateful, regardless of one's achievements.

Resilience is another key lesson from Payton's life. He faced challenges and setbacks, both on and off the field, but always demonstrated an ability to bounce back stronger. His resilience in overcoming obstacles, including injuries and defeats, exemplifies the importance of perseverance in the face of adversity.

Payton's commitment to giving back to the community and helping others is a testament to his character. His philanthropic work and advocacy for causes like organ donation highlight the importance of compassion and using one's talents and platform for the greater good.

Additionally, Payton's life teaches the value of sportsmanship and respect for the game and opponents. He played football with passion and intensity but always with a respect for the rules and the spirit of competition. This respect for the game and for others is a crucial lesson in integrity and fair play.

Lastly, Payton's joy for life and football serves as a reminder for individuals to find and pursue their passions. His love for the game was evident in every play, and his enthusiasm was contagious. This lesson underscores the importance of finding joy in one's pursuits and embracing life with a positive and passionate attitude.

Peyton Manning's Comeback

Early Career Achievements

Peyton Manning's early career in the NFL, prior to his injury, was marked by exceptional achievements and established him as one of the premier quarterbacks in the league. Born on March 24, 1976, in New Orleans, Louisiana, Peyton is the son of former NFL quarterback Archie Manning. He spent the majority of his career with the Indianapolis Colts before concluding it with the Denver Broncos. His journey from a highly touted draft pick to an NFL superstar is a testament to his skill, intelligence, and dedication to the sport.

Manning was selected as the first overall pick in the 1998 NFL Draft by the Indianapolis Colts. From the outset of his career, he showed signs of the remarkable player he would become. In his rookie season, despite facing the typical challenges of adjusting to the professional game, Manning demonstrated his potential, setting a record for most touchdown passes by a rookie.

Over the following years, Manning solidified his reputation as a top-tier quarterback. He was known for his exceptional understanding of the game, precision passing, and ability to read defenses. Manning's pre-snap adjustments and audibles became a signature aspect of his play, showcasing his football intelligence and leadership on the field.

Manning's tenure with the Colts was marked by numerous individual and team successes. He amassed a series of accolades, including multiple NFL MVP awards, and led the Colts to consistent playoff appearances. His relentless pursuit of excellence and meticulous preparation were key factors in both his individual success and the team's achievements.

One of Manning's most significant achievements with the Colts came in the 2006 season, where he led the team to victory in Super Bowl XLI against the Chicago Bears. This win not only gave Manning his first Super Bowl ring but also solidified his status as one of the great quarterbacks in NFL history.

Throughout his time with the Colts, Manning set numerous records and was consistently at the top of the league in various passing categories. He was the cornerstone of the Colts' offense, known for his ability to orchestrate high-scoring and efficient offensive drives. His leadership and performance on the field made him a beloved figure among Colts fans and respected by football enthusiasts everywhere.

Neck Injury and Recovery

Peyton Manning's career faced a significant challenge when he suffered a neck injury, leading to a complex and strenuous recovery process that tested his resilience and determination. This period marked a crucial turning point in his illustrious NFL career.

The injury, which became a major concern in 2011, was related to a bulging disc in Manning's neck. The discomfort and issues stemming from this injury were significant enough to affect his ability to play. In an effort to address the problem and return to his peak form, Manning underwent a series of neck surgeries. The most notable of these was a cervical neck fusion surgery, a procedure that involved joining selected bones in the neck.

The recovery process following the surgery was both rigorous and uncertain. Neck fusion surgery, particularly for a professional athlete like Manning, involved a significant risk and no guarantee of returning to the previous level of performance. Manning's rehabilitation process was comprehensive, involving not just the physical aspects of recovery, but also the mental and emotional challenges that come with being away from the sport.

During his recovery, Manning faced the daunting task of retraining his body and regaining his strength. This process was arduous and required immense patience, as Manning had to slowly rebuild his neck strength and reacquaint his body with the rigors of playing professional football. His rehabilitation involved specialized exercises, physical therapy, and a gradual return to football-related activities.

The uncertainty of recovery was not just physical. Manning's future with the Indianapolis Colts, the team he had led for over a decade, became unclear. The combination of his injury, recovery, and the team's performance led to difficult decisions for both Manning and the Colts' management.

Despite these challenges, Manning's determination and work ethic during his recovery were exemplary. He remained focused on his goal of returning to the NFL, even in the face of adversity and doubt. This period of recovery not only tested his physical strength but also showcased his mental toughness and unwavering commitment to the sport he loved.

Joining the Denver Broncos

Peyton Manning's transition to the Denver Broncos marked a significant chapter in his NFL career, presenting new challenges and opportunities for the veteran quarterback. After an illustrious tenure with the

Indianapolis Colts, Manning's move to Denver in 2012 was both a fresh start and a test of his ability to excel in a new environment, particularly following his recovery from neck surgery.

Manning's departure from the Colts was a momentous and emotional decision, influenced by the uncertainty surrounding his injury and the Colts' positioning for future success. As the Colts chose to rebuild with a new, younger quarterback, Manning was released, making him a free agent. This development was a turning point in his career, closing the chapter on his storied history with the Colts.

Choosing to join the Denver Broncos, Manning embarked on a journey with a team that had seen potential in him despite the risks associated with his recent injury. The Broncos, led by executive John Elway, believed in Manning's ability to lead and elevate the team, providing him with an opportunity to prove that he could still perform at an elite level.

Manning's initial challenges with the Broncos were multifaceted. Firstly, there was the physical aspect of proving that he could still play post-surgery. The football world watched with anticipation to see if Manning could regain his arm strength and durability, critical aspects of his quarterback play. There was also the challenge of adapting to a new team, system, and coaching staff, which required building chemistry with new teammates and learning new offensive schemes.

Additionally, there was the pressure of high expectations. Manning's reputation as one of the greatest quarterbacks in NFL history meant that his performance with the Broncos would be closely scrutinized. Fans and analysts were eager to see if he could replicate his success in a new setting and lead the Broncos to championship contention.

Despite these challenges, Manning approached his tenure with the Broncos with characteristic diligence and commitment. He immersed himself in learning the team's playbook, developing a rapport with his receivers, and understanding the dynamics of the Broncos' offense. His leadership and experience were immediate assets to the team, and he quickly began to make an impact on and off the field.

Winning the Super Bowl

Peyton Manning's tenure with the Denver Broncos reached a pinnacle of success with the triumphant victory in Super Bowl 50, a moment that served as the culmination of his remarkable comeback in the NFL. This achievement not only added another illustrious chapter to his career but also firmly established his legacy as one of the greatest quarterbacks in the history of the sport.

Super Bowl 50, played on February 7, 2016, saw the Broncos face off against the Carolina Panthers. Leading up to the game, there was much speculation about Manning's performance, given his age and the injuries he had overcome. However, Manning's leadership and experience proved invaluable in the high-stakes environment of the Super Bowl.

In the game, Manning demonstrated his strategic acumen, managing the offense effectively and making key plays when needed. While his statistical performance in the game was not among his most impressive, his ability to guide the team, make crucial decisions, and capitalize on the Panthers' mistakes was pivotal. His calm demeanor under pressure and his game management skills were critical components of the Broncos' strategy.

The Broncos' victory in Super Bowl 50 was a testament to the team's overall strength, particularly their formidable defense, which played a significant role in securing the win. The defense's ability to contain the Panthers' potent offense and create turnovers was key to the Broncos' success. Manning's role as a leader and a steadying influence on the team was evident throughout the game.

Manning's second Super Bowl win, and the first with the Broncos, was a significant personal triumph. It marked his return to the pinnacle of NFL success after a period of physical and professional challenges. The victory was seen by many as a validation of his resilience, skill, and determination, solidifying his status as an all-time great.

Work Ethic and Perseverance

Peyton's successful comeback after a career-threatening neck injury and subsequent transition to the Denver Broncos was underpinned by his extraordinary work ethic and perseverance. These qualities, which had been hallmarks of his career from the beginning, played a pivotal role in helping him overcome the challenges posed by his injury and return to the apex of NFL competition.

Manning's work ethic was legendary throughout his career. Known for being the first to arrive and the last to leave during practice sessions, he demonstrated an unwavering commitment to refining his skills and understanding of the game. After his neck surgery, this dedication became even more critical. Manning invested countless hours in rehabilitation, working diligently with medical professionals and trainers to regain his physical strength and conditioning. He approached his recovery with the same meticulous attention to detail that he applied to game preparation, leaving no stone unturned in his quest to return to the field.

Perseverance was another key factor in Manning's comeback. The uncertainty and physical challenges that followed his surgery would have daunted many, but Manning faced them with a steadfast resolve. He confronted setbacks during his rehabilitation process with a positive mindset, consistently focusing on his goal to return to playing at a high level. His determination during this period was a testament to his mental toughness and resilience.

Manning's ability to adapt and adjust was also crucial in overcoming his injury. He recognized the need to modify his playing style to accommodate his physical limitations post-surgery. This adaptability was evident in his play with the Broncos, where he often relied more on his mental acuity, experience, and strategic thinking than on pure physical prowess. Manning's capacity to adapt not only demonstrated his football intelligence but also his willingness to evolve as a player.

Furthermore, Manning's leadership and positive attitude were invaluable assets during his recovery. He maintained a leadership role with his team, even when he was unable to play, providing guidance and support to his teammates. His positive presence and unwavering spirit uplifted those around him and reinforced the collective resolve of the team.

Inspiration and Legacy

Peyton Manning's remarkable comeback in the NFL, culminating in a Super Bowl victory with the Denver Broncos, serves as a profound source of inspiration and cements his legacy as a symbol of resilience and dedication. His journey offers valuable lessons on the power of perseverance and the importance of commitment in the face of adversity.

Manning's comeback story teaches that resilience is a key ingredient in overcoming challenges. Facing a potentially career-ending injury and undergoing multiple surgeries, he encountered significant physical and psychological hurdles. However, his relentless determination and unwavering spirit in the face of these challenges exemplify true resilience. This aspect of his journey is particularly inspiring, demonstrating that with grit and perseverance, it's possible to surmount even the most daunting obstacles.

The dedication Manning showed during his recovery and transition to the Broncos highlights the importance of a strong work ethic and commitment to one's goals. His meticulous approach to rehabilitation, his relentless pursuit of physical and mental readiness, and his adaptation to a new team environment underscore the value of dedication in achieving success. Manning's journey is a testament to the fact that success is often a result of hard work and persistence, as much as it is of innate talent.

Manning's legacy also extends to the inspiration he provides for athletes and individuals facing their own setbacks and challenges. His story is a reminder that setbacks can be turned into comebacks with the right mindset and effort. It encourages individuals to stay focused on their goals, maintain a positive attitude, and work tirelessly towards their objectives, regardless of the obstacles they might face.

Moreover, Manning's comeback and ultimate triumph with the Broncos have solidified his status as one of the greatest quarterbacks in NFL history. His legacy is not only defined by the records he set or the games he won but also by the character he displayed throughout his career, particularly during its most challenging phase. He is remembered not just as a great athlete but as an individual who embodied the principles of resilience, dedication, and sportsmanship.

The Immaculate Reception

The 1972 Playoff Game

The 1972 AFC Divisional Playoff game, which set the stage for the iconic moment known as the "Immaculate Reception," is etched in NFL history as one of the most dramatic and memorable games. Held on December 23, 1972, the game featured the Pittsburgh Steelers and the Oakland Raiders, two powerhouse teams of the era, clashing in a fiercely competitive battle.

The game took place at Three Rivers Stadium in Pittsburgh, Pennsylvania. The atmosphere was electric, with a palpable sense of anticipation among the fans. Pittsburgh, known for its passionate and loyal fan base, was buzzing with excitement, as the Steelers had made it to the playoffs for the first time in 25 years. The Raiders, on the other hand, were an established force in the league, having been playoff contenders consistently in the preceding years.

The game itself was a defensive struggle, characterized by hard hits and a tactical battle between two well-matched teams. Both the Steelers and the Raiders showcased their defensive prowess, making it difficult for either offense to gain significant ground. The scoring was minimal, reflecting the intensity and toughness of the play.

As the game progressed, the tension mounted, with each team understanding the high stakes of a playoff victory. The Steelers, led by coach Chuck Noll, were looking to make a statement in their first playoff appearance in decades. The Raiders, under the leadership of coach John Madden, were determined to continue their legacy of success.

Heading into the final moments of the game, the Steelers were trailing the Raiders by a single point, with the score at 7-6. The situation seemed dire for Pittsburgh, as they faced a fourth down with only 22 seconds left on the clock. The Steelers' hopes of advancing in the playoffs were hanging by a thread, setting the scene for one of the most extraordinary and debated plays in NFL history.

The Play

The scene was set with the Pittsburgh Steelers in a desperate situation, facing a fourth-and-10 on their own 40-yard line, with only 22 seconds remaining in the game and trailing the Oakland Raiders 7-6. Steelers quarterback Terry Bradshaw took the snap and dropped back to pass under heavy pressure from the Raiders' defense. As the Raiders' defenders closed in, Bradshaw unleashed a desperate throw downfield towards running back John "Frenchy" Fuqua.

As the ball approached Fuqua, he collided with Raiders safety Jack Tatum, known for his hard-hitting style. The ball ricocheted off one of the players - it remains a subject of debate whether it hit Fuqua, Tatum, or both - and took an improbable bounce back towards the line of scrimmage.

In a stroke of extraordinary luck and timing, Steelers rookie running back Franco Harris, who had initially been blocking on the play, reacted swiftly to the deflected ball. Harris scooped up the ball just inches from the turf and took off down the sideline. With Raiders players in pursuit, Harris sprinted 42 yards to the end zone, scoring the game-winning touchdown as time expired.

The play immediately sparked a frenzy in Three Rivers Stadium. Steelers fans erupted in jubilation, hardly believing the miraculous turn of events. On the field, players and coaches were equally astonished. The Steelers celebrated the incredible play, while the

Raiders stood in disbelief, some protesting that the play had been illegal. Under the NFL rules at the time, a pass could not be legally caught by an offensive player if it first bounced off another offensive player, but could if it bounced off a defensive player.

The officials conferred for several minutes, adding to the tension and drama. Finally, they ruled the play a touchdown, cementing the Steelers' 13-7 victory and sending them to the AFC Championship Game.

The "Immaculate Reception" has since become a legendary moment in NFL lore. It is celebrated by Steelers fans as a miraculous and pivotal play in the franchise's history,  while for Raiders fans, it remains a controversial and painful memory. The play's name, coined by Steelers fans and the media, reflects its almost miraculous nature, and it continues to be a subject of fascination and debate among football enthusiasts.

Controversy and Analysis

The central controversy revolved around the then-existing NFL rule, which stated that a pass could not be legally caught by an offensive player if it first bounced off another offensive player. The ambiguity arose from whether the ball, thrown by Terry Bradshaw, first made contact with Steelers' running back Frenchy Fuqua or Raiders' safety Jack Tatum, or both. If the ball had only hit Fuqua, the play would have been illegal. However, if it had touched Tatum or both players, Harris' catch would be legal.

No conclusive video evidence exists to clarify this point definitively, as the available footage did not provide a clear angle on the crucial moment of the play. This lack of definitive evidence has led to ongoing debates among fans, players, and analysts. Raiders fans and players, in particular, have often contended that the play should have been ruled illegal, believing that the ball only contacted Fuqua.

The play has been dissected and analyzed from multiple angles, with various experts and enthusiasts offering their interpretations. Technological advancements have allowed for enhanced reviews of the play, but even with these tools, a definitive conclusion remains elusive. The play's mystery is compounded by the participants' accounts, as both Fuqua and Tatum provided ambiguous or conflicting statements over the years.

The controversy surrounding the "Immaculate Reception" also highlights the evolution of NFL rules and officiating. The play was a catalyst for discussions about instant replay and the need for clearer rules regarding possession and deflections. In many ways, the play's ambiguous nature exposed the limitations of officiating at the time and the need for technological aid in making accurate calls.

Furthermore, the "Immaculate Reception" has a symbolic significance beyond the controversy. For Steelers fans, it's a symbol of a miraculous turn of fortune, marking the beginning of a successful era in the franchise's history. For Raiders fans, it's often viewed as a symbol of injustice and a turning point in a rivalry marked by intense competition.

Impact on the Steelers and NFL

For the Pittsburgh Steelers, the play marked a turning point in their history. Prior to this moment, the Steelers had experienced limited success, with few playoff appearances and no championship victories. The "Immaculate Reception" seemed to catalyze a change in fortune for the team. It occurred during a critical playoff game and led to the Steelers' victory, propelling them into the AFC Championship Game. This play is often seen as the beginning of a golden era for the Steelers, who would go on to become one of the most successful franchises in the NFL in the 1970s.

The play's impact extended beyond that single season, contributing to the development of a winning culture within the Steelers organization. It helped build confidence and a sense of destiny, elements that played a decisive role in the team's subsequent successes, including four Super Bowl victories in the next six years. The "Immaculate Reception" symbolized a shift in the Steelers' identity from perennial underdogs to dominant contenders.

In the broader context of the NFL, the play holds a special place in the league's history due to its dramatic and improbable nature. It is frequently featured in discussions about the greatest and most memorable moments in football, capturing the imagination of fans and players alike. The play's significance is reflected in its enduring presence in NFL lore, where it continues to be a subject of fascination and debate.

The "Immaculate Reception" also had implications for the NFL in terms of rules and officiating. The controversy surrounding the play highlighted the need for clearer rules and eventually contributed to the development and refinement of instant replay technology. This shift towards using technology to aid in officiating decisions can be traced back, in part, to the ambiguity and debate sparked by this iconic play.

Additionally, the play has become a cultural touchstone, transcending the sport itself. It is referenced in various forms of media and is part of the collective memory of American football. The "Immaculate Reception" serves as a reminder of the unpredictability of sports and the extraordinary moments that can arise in the heat of competition.

Symbol of Hope and Luck

The play is often viewed as a symbol of luck or serendipity. The way the ball ricocheted off the players and landed perfectly for Franco Harris making the catch was a once-in-a-lifetime occurrence, illustrating how elements of chance can significantly influence defining outcomes. For many, the "Immaculate Reception" encapsulates the idea that, sometimes, success involves an element of luck, beyond skill and preparation.

However, the play also epitomizes the importance of readiness and the ability to seize opportunities. While luck played a part in how the events unfolded, it was Harris' alertness and quick reaction that ultimately made the difference. His ability to capitalize on the unexpected chance illustrates the significance of being prepared to act when opportunities arise. Harris' response to the play serves as a lesson in staying focused, being adaptable, and making the most of unforeseen circumstances.

For the Steelers and their fans, the "Immaculate Reception" has become a symbol of hope. It represents the idea that no matter how dire the situation may seem, there is always the possibility of a positive turn of events. This message of hope has resonated with the Steelers' fan base and has become a part of the team's identity.

Moreover, the play is often invoked as a metaphor for resilience and perseverance. It signifies that even in moments of uncertainty or when the odds seem insurmountable, determination and readiness can lead to remarkable achievements. This aspect of the play is particularly inspiring, offering a message of encouragement to persist in the face of challenges.

In the broader context of sports and beyond, the "Immaculate Reception" serves as a reminder of the unpredictable nature of life and the potential for extraordinary moments to occur. It encourages both athletes and individuals to remain vigilant for opportunities and underscores the notion that luck, when combined with preparedness and action, can lead to incredible outcomes.

Legacy in Sports Lore

In the realm of football folklore, the "Immaculate Reception" is celebrated as one of the most miraculous and unforgettable plays ever. It has become a staple of NFL history, often featured in highlight reels, documentaries, and discussions about the greatest moments in the sport. The play's dramatic nature, the high stakes involved, and the controversy surrounding it have contributed to its enduring appeal and intrigue.

The legacy of the "Immaculate Reception" is also evident in its influence on the culture of football. It has become a symbol of the unexpected and exhilarating nature of the sport, where a single play can change the course of a game, a season, or even a franchise's history. The play is a reminder of why fans love football - for its capacity to produce moments of sheer wonder and disbelief.

Moreover, the play has a special significance for the Pittsburgh Steelers and their fans. It is seen as a pivotal turning point in the franchise's history, marking the beginning of a period of dominance in the NFL. The "Immaculate Reception" is woven into the fabric of the Steelers' identity and is a source of pride and tradition for the team and its supporters.

The play's legacy extends to the players involved, particularly Franco Harris, who made the miraculous catch. Harris' career and legacy are inextricably linked to this moment, which showcased his athleticism and instinctive play. The "Immaculate Reception" has become a defining highlight of his career, remembered and celebrated by football fans around the world.

In addition, the "Immaculate Reception" continues to be a subject of fascination and debate among football enthusiasts. The play's controversial nature has sparked endless discussions and analyses, adding to its mythic status. It serves as a conversation starter and a point of connection for fans, fostering a sense of community and shared history.

Sarah Fuller's Historic Kick

Background

Sarah Fuller's historic journey to a groundbreaking moment in football began with her career in another sport: soccer. Fuller's background as a soccer player laid the foundation for her eventual transition into football history, showcasing her athletic skills and pioneering spirit.

Born on June 20, 1999, in Wylie, Texas, Fuller grew up with a passion for soccer, dedicating herself to the sport from a young age. Her talent and hard work in soccer led her to play at the collegiate level, where she became a key player for the Vanderbilt University women's soccer team. As a goalkeeper for Vanderbilt, Fuller demonstrated remarkable skills, including agility, strong decision-making, and leadership on the field. These qualities were pivotal in her soccer career and would later become instrumental in her historic transition to football.

During her time with the Vanderbilt soccer team, Fuller was known for her competitiveness and work ethic. She played an integral role in the team's defense, consistently delivering performances that helped secure victories and uphold the team's competitive standing. Her ability to perform under pressure and maintain composure in high-stakes situations was a testament to her athletic prowess and mental toughness.

Fuller's success in soccer was marked by team achievements and personal accolades, reflecting her impact as a player. She was part of a Vanderbilt team that made significant strides in collegiate soccer, contributing to its defensive strength. Her leadership qualities were also recognized by her teammates and coaches, as she often stepped up in crucial moments to guide and motivate the team.

Transition to Football

In the fall of 2020, the Vanderbilt football team found itself in a challenging situation due to the COVID-19 pandemic. Several of the team's specialists, including kickers, were unavailable for a game against the Missouri Tigers due to COVID-19 protocols. This situation led the football team's coaching staff to look for alternatives within the university's athletic programs.

Aware of Fuller's accomplishments as a goalkeeper for the Vanderbilt women's soccer team, the football coaches recognized potential in her strong kicking ability. They approached Fuller with the opportunity to join the football team as a kicker. Fuller, fresh off her participation in the SEC Championship with the soccer team, accepted the offer, seeing it as a chance to contribute to another Vanderbilt sports team and embrace a new athletic challenge.

Fuller's decision to join the football team was a significant one, not just for her but for the sport of football. By agreeing to play as a kicker, she was set to break barriers in an overwhelmingly male-dominated sport. Her willingness to step into this new role demonstrated her courage and commitment to pushing boundaries in collegiate sports.

Fuller's transition to football involved a rapid adjustment period. She had to acclimate to the different techniques and dynamics of football kicking, as opposed to soccer goalkeeping. Her practice sessions with the football team were focused on honing her skills for kickoffs and point-after attempts, translating her soccer skills into football proficiency.

The Historic Game

Sarah Fuller's historic moment in football occurred on November 28, 2020, during a game that would etch her name in the annals of sports history. This game, where she took to the field as a kicker for the Vanderbilt University football team, marked a groundbreaking moment in the traditionally male-dominated sport of college football.

The game was an SEC matchup between Vanderbilt and the University of Missouri. Held at Memorial Stadium in Columbia, Missouri, the game drew significant attention, not just for the competition itself, but for the anticipation of Fuller's participation. Her presence on the roster had made national headlines, sparking conversations about gender barriers in sports.

Fuller's opportunity came on November 28, after halftime. Vanderbilt, trailing in the game, turned to Fuller to execute the second-half kickoff. This moment was laden with significance, as it marked the first time a woman played in a Power Five conference football game, the highest level of college football in the United States.

Dressed in Vanderbilt gear with the words "Play Like a Girl" on the back of her helmet, a nod to the slogan promoting female participation in sports, Fuller approached the kickoff with confidence. She executed a perfectly-placed squib kick that was downed by Missouri at their 35-yard line, ensuring no return. While the kick was tactically planned, it was also symbolic, representing a barrier-breaking moment in the sport.

Fuller's historic play was met with widespread recognition and celebration. Her teammates and coaches, along with the spectators, acknowledged the significance of the moment. The impact of her participation transcended the game's score or outcome, marking a milestone for gender inclusion and diversity in sports.

Her participation in this game was not only a personal achievement for Fuller but also a monumental step forward for women in sports. It challenged long-standing gender norms and inspired countless young girls and women, demonstrating that opportunities in sports should not be limited by gender.

Challenges and Reaction

One of the primary challenges Fuller faced was the physical and technical transition from soccer to football. Kicking a football, especially in a game situation, required adapting her soccer skills to the nuances of football, a challenge she embraced with determination. Additionally, the intense scrutiny and pressure that came with being in the national spotlight presented a mental and emotional challenge. Fuller had to navigate this while staying focused on her performance.

There was also the challenge of entering a male-dominated sport, where female participation at this level was unprecedented. Fuller had to integrate into the team and adapt to a new sporting environment, all under the watchful eyes of the media and the public. This situation required not only physical skill and mental toughness but also a strong sense of self-confidence and resilience.

The public reaction to Fuller's participation was mixed, though largely positive and supportive. Many people, including prominent figures in sports and other fields, praised her for breaking barriers and setting an example for young girls and women. Her appearance was seen as a significant step forward for gender equality in sports, inspiring countless aspiring female athletes.

However, Fuller's role as a trailblazer also attracted criticism and skepticism from some quarters. Critics questioned the quality of her play and the motives behind her inclusion on the team. This criticism was part of the broader discourse about the place of women in traditionally male-dominated sports.

Fuller's teammates and the Vanderbilt community largely supported her. They recognized the courage and commitment it took for her to step into this new role and appreciated the attention and conversation her participation brought to the team and the university.

Additionally, Fuller's achievement sparked discussions in the wider sports community about opportunities for women in sports, challenging traditional gender norms and highlighting the need for greater inclusivity. Her historic kick was not just a personal achievement but a moment that prompted reflection on the progress and potential in women's sports.

Gender Barriers in Sports

Fuller's accomplishment is particularly noteworthy considering the landscape of college football, a sport that has traditionally been an exclusively male domain, especially at the Power Five conference level. Her presence on the field challenged the preconceived notions about the roles and capabilities of female athletes in such a high-profile and physically demanding sport. It sent a powerful message that skill and talent are not confined by gender.

The significance of Fuller's achievement extends beyond her personal accomplishment; it symbolizes the broader struggle for gender equality in sports. Her participation in a college football game highlighted the disparities that still exist in athletic opportunities and recognition between men and women. It brought to light the ongoing need to advocate for equal opportunities for female athletes in all sports, including those traditionally dominated by men.

Fuller's role in breaking gender barriers also served as an inspiration for young girls and women with aspirations in sports, demonstrating that the boundaries of what is possible are continually expanding. Her story is a vivid example that can encourage young female athletes to pursue their sporting ambitions, even in fields where they may be underrepresented.

Furthermore, her achievement prompted discussions about how sports organizations, from youth leagues to professional levels, can create more inclusive environments. It underscored the importance of providing support systems, resources, and equitable opportunities for female athletes. Fuller's participation in a football game is a reminder of the need for ongoing advocacy and action to ensure that gender does not limit access to sports and athletic development.

In the larger societal context, Fuller's historic kick resonates beyond the realm of sports, contributing to the dialogue about gender roles and equality in various sectors. It illustrates how sports can be a catalyst for social change and a platform for challenging stereotypes and advocating for equality.

Role Model and Inspiration

Sarah Fuller's story transcends the realm of sports, positioning her as a role model and source of inspiration for young girls and boys alike. Her groundbreaking achievement in college football exemplifies qualities such as courage, perseverance, and the willingness to challenge norms, making her an influential figure for the younger generation.

For young girls, Fuller's journey is a powerful illustration of breaking gender barriers and challenging societal expectations. Her success in a male-dominated sport provides tangible proof that girls can aspire to and achieve greatness in any field they choose, regardless of traditional gender roles. Fuller's story sends a message of empowerment, encouraging young girls to pursue their passions and dreams with confidence, even in areas where they may be underrepresented.

Boys, too, can draw inspiration from Fuller's story. It teaches them the importance of inclusivity and respect for diversity in all aspects of life, including sports. Seeing a woman excel in a role traditionally held by men can help young boys understand and appreciate the value of equality and the need to support and celebrate achievements irrespective of gender. Fuller's story can contribute to shaping a more equitable mindset in boys from a young age.

Moreover, Fuller's embodiment of resilience and determination in the face of challenges is a universal lesson. Her ability to step into a high-pressure situation, adapt to a new environment, and perform with composure is inspirational for all young people. It underscores the virtues of hard work, dedication, and staying focused on one's goals, regardless of the obstacles.

Fuller also represents the importance of seizing opportunities and being open to new experiences. Her willingness to take on a challenge outside her comfort zone is a valuable lesson in personal growth and exploration. This aspect of her story encourages young people to be open-minded and courageous in exploring their own potential and interests.

In addition to her achievements on the field, Fuller's positive attitude, team spirit, and advocacy for inclusivity make her a role model off the field. Her engagement with initiatives like "Play Like a Girl" and her advocacy for female participation in sports serve as further inspiration, highlighting her commitment to making a difference beyond her athletic accomplishments.

Sarah Fuller's role as a model and inspiration is significant for young girls and boys. Her story is a compelling example of challenging gender norms, demonstrating resilience, and embracing opportunities. It inspires young people to pursue their dreams with determination and confidence, promotes inclusivity and equality, and highlights the importance of hard work and a positive attitude in achieving one's goals.

The Ice Bowl

Setting the Stage

The 1967 NFL Championship game, famously known as the "Ice Bowl," is one of the most legendary games in the history of the league, remembered particularly for its brutal weather conditions and the high stakes involved. Played on December 31, 1967, the game set the stage for a dramatic and enduring chapter in NFL lore.

The game was a showdown between the Green Bay Packers and the Dallas Cowboys, held at Lambeau Field in Green Bay, Wisconsin. The stakes were incredibly high, as the game would determine the National

Football League champion for the 1967 season and decide who would go on to play in Super Bowl II.

However, what made the Ice Bowl particularly infamous were the extreme weather conditions. On game day, Green Bay was gripped by a brutal cold wave. Temperatures plummeted to a bone-chilling -13 degrees Fahrenheit (-25 degrees Celsius), with the wind chill pushing it down to a staggering -48 degrees Fahrenheit (-44 degrees Celsius). These were some of the coldest conditions ever recorded for an NFL game, earning the matchup its nickname.

The frigid temperatures had a significant impact on the game. The field itself, despite having an underground heating system, froze into a hard, icy surface, earning it the moniker of "the frozen tundra." Players struggled with the cold, dealing with issues like frostbite and difficulty breathing. The icy field conditions also affected the game's play, as it was challenging for players to get traction and maintain their footing.

The atmosphere in the stadium was electric, despite the bitter cold. Fans braved the extreme temperatures to support their teams, bundled up in layers of clothing. The Packers, led by the legendary coach Vince Lombardi, were seeking their third consecutive NFL championship, adding to the game's intensity. The Cowboys, under coach Tom Landry, were aiming to dethrone the Packers and claim their first NFL title.

Gameplay in Extreme Conditions

The gameplay of the 1967 NFL Championship, known as the Ice Bowl, was profoundly affected by the extreme cold conditions, presenting unique challenges for both the Green Bay Packers and the Dallas Cowboys. The frigid temperatures and icy field significantly influenced the strategies, performance, and physical well-being of the players.

In these severe conditions, the physical toll on the players was evident. The brutal cold made it difficult for them to stay warm and maintain flexibility, affecting their speed, agility, and overall performance. Players faced the risk of frostbite, and the cold air made breathing painful, adding to the physical strain of the game. Despite wearing thermal clothing, heated benches, and other measures to combat the cold, the players were visibly affected by the extreme weather.

The icy surface of Lambeau Field, notoriously hard and slippery due to the sub-zero temperatures, altered the dynamics of the game. Players struggled for traction, leading to more slipping and falling than in typical games. This affected everything from the effectiveness of running plays to the ability of receivers and defenders to make sharp cuts. The passing game was also impacted, as quarterbacks found it challenging to grip and throw the ball accurately in the freezing conditions.

The extreme weather necessitated adjustments in game strategies. Both teams had to rely more on short, strategic plays rather than long passes or complex formations that required precise movements. The running game became more critical, though ball carriers  faced their challenges with the slippery ball and icy turf.

Defensively, players had to adjust their techniques to ensure stability and balance, as the usual quick movements and hard tackles were riskier on the frozen field. The game became as much about managing the conditions as it was about outmaneuvering the opponent.

Coaches Vince Lombardi of the Packers and Tom Landry of the Cowboys faced the challenge of adapting their game plans to the conditions. Their decisions on play-calling and player rotations were crucial in a game where endurance and resilience were as important as skill and strategy.

Key Moments and Players

One of the most pivotal figures in the game was Bart Starr, the quarterback for the Green Bay Packers. Starr's leadership and poise under pressure were critical to the Packers' offense. Despite the difficult conditions, he managed to execute plays with precision and calmness. His ability to adapt to the icy field and maintain control of the game was a testament to his skill and experience.

The game's defining moment came in its final seconds. With just 16 seconds left on the clock and the Packers trailing by three points, Starr executed one of the most famous plays in NFL history. In a gutsy call, Starr ran a quarterback sneak on the 1-yard line, successfully crossing into the end zone for the game-winning touchdown. This play, known as "the sneak," is forever etched in the annals of the NFL as a symbol of grit and determination.

Another key player in the game was Packers' running back Donny Anderson. In the treacherous conditions, Anderson's efforts were crucial in gaining hard-earned yards on the ground. His ability to navigate the icy turf and maintain possession under challenging conditions was vital for the Packers' offense.

On the defensive side, the Packers' Ray Nitschke played a significant role. His performance in the linebacker position was critical in halting the Cowboys' offense. Nitschke's leadership on the field helped galvanize the Packers' defense against the formidable Dallas team.

For the Dallas Cowboys, quarterback Don Meredith was a standout player. Meredith faced immense pressure from the Packers' defense but managed to lead his team with composure. His throws and strategic play-calling kept the Cowboys competitive throughout the game.

Wide receiver Lance Rentzel of the Cowboys also made significant contributions. Rentzel's receptions were crucial in advancing the Cowboys' offense, and his ability to make catches in the harsh conditions demonstrated his skill and adaptability.

The Ice Bowl was not just a display of individual talent but also a testament to team effort and strategic coaching. Vince Lombardi and Tom Landry, coaches for the Packers and Cowboys respectively, demonstrated their strategic prowess, making critical decisions that influenced the course of the game.

Mental and Physical Toughness

The Ice Bowl, played under some of the harshest conditions in NFL history, was a profound testament to the mental and physical toughness displayed by the players of both the Green Bay Packers and the Dallas Cowboys. The extreme cold and challenging field conditions required an extraordinary level of endurance and resilience from every player on the field.

Physically, the players were pushed to their limits. The sub-zero temperatures posed a significant challenge, affecting muscle function, agility, and overall physical performance. Players had to combat the risk of frostbite and hypothermia while engaging in intense physical activity. The ability to maintain focus on the game, execute plays, and withstand hits in such conditions demonstrated remarkable physical fortitude.

The icy field added another layer to the physical challenge. Players had to adjust their movements and tactics to avoid slips and falls, which required not only physical skill but also a heightened awareness of the playing surface. The effort to stay upright and effective in such an environment, while battling the extreme cold, spoke volumes about their physical toughness and adaptability.

Mentally, the players exhibited exceptional toughness and focus. Playing in such extreme weather conditions required a strong mental attitude. The ability to concentrate on the game, execute strategic plays, and maintain a competitive edge under such circumstances was a significant mental challenge. Players had to mentally overcome the discomfort and distractions posed by the cold, channeling their focus solely on the game.

The endurance shown by the players was also remarkable. As the game progressed, fatigue set in, exacerbated by the cold. The players' ability to continue performing at a high level, pushing through fatigue and the physical discomforts of the cold, was a testament to their stamina and endurance.

Moreover, the game required a high level of mental resilience. The pressure of a championship game, combined with the adverse weather conditions, could easily have overwhelmed the players. Yet, they demonstrated remarkable composure and mental strength, particularly in the game's critical moments, such as Bart Starr's game-winning quarterback sneak in the final seconds.

Outcome and Aftermath

The outcome of the Ice Bowl had significant and lasting implications for both the Green Bay Packers and the Dallas Cowboys, as well as for the players involved. The game, which ended with a narrow 21-17 victory for the Packers, had a profound impact on the legacy of both teams and the individuals who played in it.

For the Green Bay Packers, the victory in the Ice Bowl solidified their status as one of the NFL's most dominant teams of the era. It marked their third consecutive NFL Championship, a remarkable feat that underscored the team's prowess and the effective leadership of coach Vince Lombardi. The win also secured the Packers' place in Super Bowl II, where they would go on to achieve another victory, further cementing their legacy in the annals of football history.

The game's outcome was a pivotal moment for several Packers players. Quarterback Bart Starr, whose game-winning quarterback sneak became an iconic moment in NFL history, enhanced his reputation as a clutch performer and one of the greatest quarterbacks of his time. The resilience and toughness demonstrated by the Packers' players in the Ice Bowl added to their individual legacies and the team's lore.

For the Dallas Cowboys, the loss was a bitter pill to swallow. Coming so close to victory only to fall short in the final moments was a devastating outcome. However, the game also served as a catalyst for the Cowboys, who would go on to become a dominant force in the NFL in the ensuing years. The experience of the Ice Bowl, while painful, contributed to the team's growth and eventual success, including multiple Super Bowl victories in the 1970s.

The Ice Bowl also had a profound personal impact on the players. The physical and mental demands of the game, played in such extreme conditions, were a true test of endurance and resilience. For many players, the Ice Bowl remained one of the most memorable and defining moments of their careers. The game's legacy continued to be a point of reflection for the players, as they recalled the challenges and triumphs of that historic day.

In the broader context of the NFL, the Ice Bowl became a symbol of the harsh and unpredictable nature of football, as well as the incredible perseverance and determination required to succeed in the sport. The game's dramatic finish and the extreme weather conditions in which it was played have ensured its place in NFL folklore, often referenced in discussions about the greatest games in football history.

Lessons in Resilience

The Ice Bowl, with its extreme weather conditions and high-stakes gameplay, offers valuable lessons in resilience, teaching how to cope with and overcome adverse situations. This legendary game serves as a powerful metaphor for the challenges faced in sports and life, highlighting the virtues of perseverance, adaptability, and mental fortitude.

One key lesson from the Ice Bowl is the importance of preparation and adaptability in the face of adversity. The players and coaches had to adjust their strategies and techniques to contend with the extreme cold and icy field. This adaptability is a vital skill, not just in sports, but in any challenging situation. It teaches that while one cannot always control the circumstances, the ability to adapt and find ways to succeed within those constraints is essential.

The game also exemplifies the importance of mental toughness. The players had to maintain focus and composure despite the physical discomfort and the high-pressure environment. This mental resilience is critical in overcoming difficult situations. It shows the power of a positive mindset and determination in facing challenges, whether on the football field, in personal endeavors, or in professional pursuits.

Another lesson from the Ice Bowl is the significance of teamwork and collective effort in overcoming adversity. The challenging conditions of the game required players to rely on each other and work together cohesively. This sense of teamwork underscores the value of collaboration and support in difficult times. It demonstrates that often, the best way to overcome adversity is by leaning on and working with others.

The players' endurance and persistence in the Ice Bowl are also instructive. The ability to keep pushing forward, even when conditions are harsh and the odds seem insurmountable, is a testament to the human spirit. This endurance is a powerful lesson in not giving up, showing that persistence and hard work can lead to success, even in the most daunting circumstances.

Finally, the Ice Bowl teaches the value of perspective in facing challenges. For the players and fans, the game was more than just a contest; it was a test of character and a memorable experience that lasted a lifetime. This perspective helps in understanding that sometimes, the journey and the lessons learned in facing adversity can be as valuable as the outcome itself.

Derrick Coleman's Inspiring Journey

Early Life and Challenges

Derrick Coleman's inspiring journey to the NFL is marked by his remarkable resilience and determination in the face of significant challenges. Born on October 18, 1990, in West Los Angeles, California, Coleman faced a major life challenge from a young age: he was diagnosed with a genetic hearing impairment when he was just three years old. This condition left him legally deaf, presenting a unique set of challenges that he would navigate throughout his life and athletic career.

Growing up, Coleman wore hearing aids and learned to read lips to communicate effectively. His hearing impairment posed various obstacles, particularly in social and educational settings, where he often had to contend with misunderstandings and a lack of awareness about his condition. Despite these challenges, Coleman showed an early resilience and a determination not to let his hearing impairment define him or limit his potential.

His journey into football began in his school years, where his talent and passion for the sport became evident. Coleman faced additional challenges on the football field due to his hearing impairment. The noisy environment of football games and practices made communication difficult, as it was hard to hear calls and signals. However, he adapted by using his hearing aids and relying on his ability to read lips and pay close attention to visual cues.

Coleman's early life was not just about overcoming the challenges of being deaf; it was also about proving his abilities and worth both on and off the field. He worked tirelessly to improve his football skills, showing a natural aptitude for the sport. His dedication and hard work were evident, as he excelled in high school football, becoming a standout player.

His determination to succeed despite his hearing impairment was a source of inspiration to those around him. Coleman didn't view his deafness as a disability, but rather as a challenge to be overcome. This mindset would be a guiding principle throughout his life, driving him to break barriers and achieve his dreams against the odds.

Path to the NFL

After a successful high school football career, Coleman attended the University of California, Los Angeles (UCLA), where he played as a fullback for the Bruins. At UCLA, he demonstrated his formidable skills on the field, combining power and agility to become a key player in the team's offense. Coleman's time in college was not just about showcasing his athletic abilities; it also involved honing his skills to communicate effectively on the field despite his hearing impairment.

Coleman's performance at UCLA set the stage for his entry into professional football. However, his path to the NFL was not straightforward. In the 2012 NFL Draft, Coleman went undrafted, a setback that would have deterred many but only fueled his determination. His response to this disappointment was to work even harder, remaining steadfast in his goal to play in the NFL.

Coleman's perseverance paid off when he signed as an undrafted free agent with the Minnesota Vikings. Although his time with the Vikings was short-lived, he did not give up on his dream. He continued to train and improve, showcasing the tenacity that had characterized his journey so far.

His breakthrough came when he signed with the Seattle Seahawks. With the Seahawks, Coleman's career took a significant turn. He became an integral part of the team, contributing both on special teams and as a fullback. His ability to read the game, combined with his physical prowess, made him a valuable asset to the team.

Coleman's presence in the NFL was groundbreaking. As the first legally deaf offensive player in the NFL, he broke significant barriers and served as an inspiration to many. His journey to the NFL highlighted not just his exceptional talent as a football player but also the importance of resilience, adaptability, and sheer determination in overcoming challenges.

Overcoming Communication Barriers

Derrick Coleman's journey in the NFL was not only remarkable for his athletic prowess but also for how he adeptly overcame communication barriers related to his deafness. His ability to adapt to these challenges in the professional football environment is a significant aspect of his inspiring story.

In the fast-paced and often noisy world of NFL games, effective communication is fundamental. For Coleman, who is legally deaf, this presented a unique set of challenges. He tackled these obstacles head-on, using a combination of technology, visual cues, and personal strategies to ensure effective communication on and off the field.

One of the key adaptations Coleman made was the use of specially designed hearing aids. These devices were tailored to withstand the rigors of a football game, including the physical contact and the sweat and moisture of intense physical exertion. The hearing aids helped amplify sounds, allowing Coleman to hear calls and signals better.

In addition to technological aids, Coleman heavily relied on lip-reading to understand his teammates and coaches. This skill, which he had honed since childhood, was invaluable in helping him pick up instructions and cues during games and practices. His ability to read lips was complemented by his teammates and coaches, who were mindful of facing him when speaking to ensure clear communication.

Coleman also utilized visual signals on the field. He paid close attention to the physical cues and hand signals from his teammates and coaches. This visual communication was crucial during loud games where hearing aids were less effective due to the overwhelming noise in the stadium.

Another important aspect of Coleman's communication strategy was his proactive approach. He made it a point to familiarize himself thoroughly with the playbook and game plans. This preparation meant he often knew what to expect on the field, reducing the need for on-the-spot verbal communication.

The Seattle Seahawks, in turn, showed commendable inclusivity in accommodating Coleman's needs. The team and staff embraced the challenge of effective communication, demonstrating an awareness and sensitivity to Coleman's situation. This collaborative effort was a testament to the team's cohesion and adaptability.

Success with the Seahawks

During his stint with the Seahawks, Coleman established himself as a reliable and versatile player. He excelled in the role of a fullback and was a key contributor on special teams. His physicality, combined with his keen understanding of the game, made him an asset in blocking schemes and in executing plays that required precision and force. Coleman's ability to perform various roles showcased his adaptability and commitment to the team's success.

Coleman's contributions were not limited to his on-field performance. He was also an integral part of the team's locker room dynamics, bringing an inspiring presence and a positive attitude. His journey to the NFL and his ability to overcome challenges resonated with his teammates, making him a motivational figure within the Seahawks organization.

His most significant contribution came during the Seahawks' successful 2013 season, which culminated in their victory in Super Bowl XLVIII. Coleman's role in this championship run was decisive. He contributed significantly on special teams and as a fullback, helping to bolster the Seahawks' powerful offense and effective special teams unit. His performance in the Super Bowl and throughout the season was a reflection of his hard work and dedication to his craft.

In Super Bowl XLVIII, held on February 2, 2014, against the Denver Broncos, Coleman's contributions, though not headline-grabbing, were vital to the team's dominant performance. The Seahawks' victory in the Super Bowl was a team effort, and Coleman's role was a testament to the importance of every player's contribution, regardless of the prominence of their role.

Off the field, Coleman's presence in the Super Bowl also carried significant symbolic weight. As the first legally deaf offensive player to participate in a Super Bowl, he broke barriers and set an inspiring example. His participation in the Super Bowl was a moment of pride not just for him but also for the deaf and hard-of-hearing community, showcasing the possibilities for athletes with disabilities at the highest levels of sports.

Advocacy and Impact

Coleman has used his platform as a professional athlete to shed light on the challenges faced by the deaf and hard-of-hearing community. He has been vocal about his own experiences, sharing his story to inspire and empower others who face similar challenges. By openly discussing the obstacles he overcame, Coleman has helped to demystify hearing impairments and reduce the stigma often associated with them.

Beyond sharing his personal story, Coleman has been actively involved in various initiatives and organizations that support the deaf community. He has participated in events and campaigns aimed at providing resources and support for individuals with hearing impairments. His involvement in these activities has helped to raise funds, increase awareness, and provide practical support to those in need.

One significant aspect of Coleman's advocacy is his emphasis on the importance of access to education and resources for the deaf and hard-of-hearing. He has highlighted the need for better communication tools, educational opportunities, and support systems that enable individuals with hearing impairments to reach their full potential.

Coleman's impact as an advocate is also noticeable in his capacity as a role model and a source of inspiration. His success in the NFL has shown that hearing impairments do not define a person's capabilities or limit their potential for success. He has become a symbol of resilience and determination, encouraging others to pursue their dreams regardless of the challenges they face.

Moreover, Coleman's advocacy extends to encouraging inclusivity and diversity in sports and beyond. He has been a voice for the importance of creating environments where people with disabilities are included and can thrive. His journey challenges stereotypes and promotes a more inclusive perspective in sports, education, and all areas of society.

Inspiration and Determination

Derrick Coleman's inspiring journey from a young boy with a hearing impairment to a successful NFL player is a powerful narrative that teaches valuable lessons about overcoming personal challenges and achieving dreams. His story exemplifies the virtues of determination, resilience, and the unyielding pursuit of one's goals, regardless of the obstacles.

One of the key lessons from Coleman's story is the importance of self-belief and determination. Facing the challenge of being legally deaf in a sport where communication is crucial, Coleman never let his hearing impairment define him or limit his aspirations. His unwavering belief in his abilities and his determination to succeed in football demonstrate that personal challenges can be overcome with perseverance and a strong sense of self-confidence.

Coleman's journey also highlights the significance of resilience. Throughout his life, he encountered various obstacles, from being undrafted in the NFL to adapting to the demands of professional football with a hearing impairment. His ability to bounce back from setbacks, to adapt and find ways to excel, serves as a lesson in resilience. It shows that challenges, whether physical or situational, can be transformed into stepping stones for success.

Another important aspect of Coleman's story is the power of hard work and preparation. His success in the NFL was not just a result of his talent but also his dedication to honing his skills and preparing himself both physically and mentally for the demands of the game. Coleman's rigorous training and meticulous preparation are examples of how hard work and dedication are critical components in achieving one's dreams.

Moreover, Coleman's story is an inspiration for individuals facing personal challenges of their own. His success serves as a powerful reminder that limitations, whether physical or otherwise, do not have to hinder one's achievements. His journey encourages others to pursue their dreams with determination, regardless of the challenges they may face.

Coleman's influence reaches beyond being a role model. For young people, particularly those with disabilities or facing significant challenges, his story is a source of motivation. It illustrates that with the right mindset, support, and hard work, it is possible to overcome adversity and achieve great things.

The Legend of Jerry Rice

Background and Early Years

Jerry Rice, widely regarded as one of the greatest wide receivers in NFL history, had a humble beginning that belied his future success in professional football. Born on October 13, 1962, in Starkville, Mississippi, Rice grew up in the small town of Crawford. His early life in rural Mississippi was far removed from the glitz and glamour of the NFL, setting the stage for a journey marked by hard work and perseverance.

Rice's introduction to football was somewhat serendipitous. During his high school years at B.L. Moor High School in Oktoc, Mississippi, his speed and athletic ability caught the attention of the school's football coach, who noticed him after Rice was caught being a prankster. His sprinting away from the school's principal demonstrated a natural athleticism that was soon harnessed on the football field.

In high school, Rice quickly developed into a standout player, displaying an early talent for catching the ball and a strong work ethic. Despite his obvious talent, he was not heavily recruited by major college football programs, primarily due to the lack of exposure at his small high school.

Rice's journey to the NFL took a significant turn when he attended Mississippi Valley State University, a small historically black university in Itta Bena. It was here that Rice's talent truly began to shine. Playing for the Delta Devils from 1981 to 1984, he set numerous NCAA records, thanks to his remarkable ability to catch and accumulate yards after the catch. His exceptional performance in college, where he displayed a unique combination of speed, agility, and precise route-running, started to draw attention from NFL scouts.

Despite his stellar college career, questions lingered about the level of competition he faced at a small university, and how well his skills would translate to the professional level. However, Rice's work ethic, combined with his natural talent, would soon quash any doubts, paving his way to an illustrious career in the NFL.

Career Highlights

Rice's professional journey began when he was drafted by the San Francisco 49ers in the first round of the 1985 NFL Draft. Despite a challenging start to his rookie season, he quickly adapted to the NFL's pace and physicality, setting the tone for what would become one of the most storied careers in football history.

One of Rice's most significant achievements is his status as the NFL's all-time leader in receiving yards. Over the course of his career, he amassed an astonishing 22,895 receiving yards, setting a standard for excellence and durability that remains unmatched. This record is a testament to his ability to perform at a high level consistently over a long period.

Rice also holds the record for the most receptions in NFL history. His total of 1,549 receptions reflects his reliability and skill in catching the ball, as well as his longevity in the league. His exceptional hand-eye coordination, precise route running, and ability to make catches in traffic were hallmarks of his playing style.

Another notable record held by Rice is the most touchdown receptions in NFL history, with 197. This remarkable achievement underscores his scoring ability and his knack for finding the end zone. Rice's combination of speed, agility, and understanding of defensive schemes made him a constant scoring threat.

Rice's career was also marked by his performances in high-stakes games. He holds the record for the most receiving yards in Super Bowl history, a testament to his ability to deliver in crucial moments. His Super Bowl performances were often game-changing, including a record-setting three touchdown receptions in Super Bowl XXIV.

In addition to his statistical achievements, what made Rice a phenomenal wide receiver was his meticulous approach to the game. He was renowned for his rigorous offseason training regimen, which included running steep hills to build endurance and strength. This commitment to conditioning contributed significantly to his longevity and productivity on the field.

Rice's ability to excel with different quarterbacks throughout his career also highlighted his adaptability and skill. He maintained his high level of play regardless of changes in the 49ers' and later teams' rosters, demonstrating his universal impact as a receiver.

Work Ethic

Rice's training regimen was famously rigorous and unconventional. He was renowned for his offseason workouts, which were both physically demanding and mentally challenging. One of the most iconic aspects of his training was his hill running. Rice would run a steep hill, known locally as "The Hill," in the San Carlos neighborhood of San Carlos, California. This grueling exercise, which he did throughout his career, was more than just a physical workout; it was a symbol of his determination and commitment to excellence. The hill runs not only built his endurance and strength but also instilled a mental toughness that became a hallmark of his career.

Beyond his physical training, Rice's dedication to perfecting his craft extended to all aspects of his role as a wide receiver. He was meticulous about studying game films, analyzing opponents' defenses, and understanding the nuances of different routes and plays. This deep understanding of the game enabled him to outsmart defenders and consistently find ways to get open.

Rice's practice sessions were known for their intensity. He treated each practice like a game, believing that the habits formed in practice translated directly to performance on the field. His attention to detail in practice, from the precision of his route running to the consistency of his catching, set a standard for the entire team.

His dedication also manifested in his approach to physical conditioning and nutrition. Rice was mindful of his diet and overall fitness, understanding the importance of maintaining peak physical condition to perform at the highest level and extend his career.

Furthermore, Rice's work ethic extended to the offseason, where he famously avoided taking extended breaks, choosing instead to maintain a high level of training. This year-round dedication ensured that he entered each season in top physical and mental shape, ready to perform at his best.

Key Games and Performances

One of Rice's most iconic performances came in Super Bowl XXIII in 1989, where the San Francisco 49ers faced the Cincinnati Bengals. In a game that was fiercely contested, Rice's contribution was monumental. He caught 11 passes for an astonishing 215 yards and scored one touchdown, playing a crucial role in the 49ers' 20-16 victory. His performance earned him the Super Bowl MVP, a rare honor for a wide receiver, and solidified his reputation for delivering in high-stakes situations.

Another notable Super Bowl performance by Rice was in Super Bowl XXIV the following year, against the Denver Broncos. Rice showcased his scoring prowess by catching three touchdown passes, contributing significantly to the 49ers' overwhelming 55-10 victory. This performance further cemented Rice's status as a key player in the 49ers' dynasty and one of the greatest receivers in Super Bowl history.

Rice's impact was not limited to Super Bowls. Throughout his career, he delivered in crucial games. A standout example is the 1994 NFC Championship game against the Dallas Cowboys. In a highly anticipated matchup, Rice made an immediate impact by scoring a 44-yard touchdown on the game's third play. His presence and performance were instrumental in the 49ers' 38-28 win, propelling them to Super Bowl XXIX.

In Super Bowl XXIX against the San Diego Chargers, Rice again proved why he was considered one of the best, catching 10 passes for 149 yards and three touchdowns. His ability to perform under pressure was on full display, helping the 49ers secure a convincing 49-26 victory.

Beyond these marquee games, Rice's career was filled with remarkable performances that showcased his consistency and dominance. He set numerous records, including most touchdowns in a single season and most receiving yards in a single game. Rice's ability to perform at an elite level, game after game, season after season, made him a constant threat on the field and a nightmare for defenses.

Impact on the Game

Rice transformed the wide receiver position through his unparalleled work ethic, route-running precision, and consistent performance. His ability to run routes with exceptional precision made him a master at creating separation from defenders. This aspect of his game, combined with his sure hands and remarkable ability to make catches in traffic, redefined what it meant to be an elite wide receiver. Rice's style of play emphasized the importance of technical skill and intelligence, in addition to physical attributes like speed and strength.

Beyond his on-field skills, Rice's approach to training and preparation had a significant impact on the position. His rigorous offseason workouts, including the notorious hill runs, demonstrated a level of dedication and commitment that was inspirational for other players. Rice showed that being a great wide receiver was not just about natural talent but also about hard work, discipline, and constant self-improvement. His training regimen became a model for wide receivers and other position players who sought to elevate their game.

Rice's influence extended to the strategic aspects of football. His ability to consistently make big plays and impact games forced teams to rethink their defensive strategies. Defenses had to account for Rice in their game plans, often requiring double coverage or specific schemes to try and contain him. This opened opportunities for other aspects of the offense, showcasing how a dominant wide receiver could change the dynamics of the game.

Furthermore, Rice's success and longevity in the NFL have inspired future generations of wide receivers. He set numerous records, many of which were considered unbreakable, creating a legacy that aspiring players sought to emulate. Rice became a role model for young athletes, not just for his achievements but for the character and professionalism he displayed throughout his career.

His influence can be seen in the way modern wide receivers approach the game. The importance of route running, maintaining peak physical condition, and studying the game are now staples for success at the position, much of which can be attributed to the standard Rice set.

Life Lessons

Jerry Rice's illustrious career and life story impart significant life lessons, particularly emphasizing the importance of hard work, dedication, and the pursuit of excellence. His journey from a modest background to becoming one of the greatest players in NFL history serves as a powerful example of these virtues.

The lesson of hard work is central to Rice's story. His relentless work ethic, both during the season and in the off-season, was a critical factor in his success. Rice's commitment to training, whether it was running challenging hill workouts or spending extra hours catching balls after practice, demonstrated that success in any field requires consistent and focused effort. His approach underscores the idea that while talent is valuable, it is hard work that often makes the difference between good and great.

Dedication is another key lesson from Rice's career. Throughout his years in the NFL, Rice remained committed to his goals, never settling for anything less than his best. He was dedicated not only to improving his physical skills but also to understanding the game's strategic aspects. This dedication extended to his diet, physical conditioning, and mental preparation, showing that true excellence requires a holistic and unwavering commitment to one's craft.

Rice's career also teaches the importance of the pursuit of excellence. He constantly set high standards for himself, striving to be the best player he could be. This pursuit was not about complacency or resting on his laurels; even after achieving significant milestones, Rice continued to push himself. His career exemplifies the idea that the pursuit of excellence is a continuous journey, not a destination.

Additionally, Rice's journey teaches resilience and the ability to overcome challenges. Facing initial difficulties in his rookie season, he demonstrated the ability to learn from mistakes and bounce back stronger. This resilience is a pivotal life lesson, emphasizing that setbacks can be opportunities for growth and improvement.

Moreover, Rice's story is an inspiration for setting and achieving goals. He had a clear vision of what he wanted to accomplish and diligently worked towards those goals. His success shows that with a clear focus and the willingness to put in the necessary effort, achieving one's dreams is possible.

The Iron Will of Brett Favre

Rise to Fame

Brett Favre's rise to fame in the NFL is a compelling story of resilience, talent, and an iron will, which saw him transform from a second-round draft pick into one of the most iconic quarterbacks in football history. His journey is marked by a combination of raw skill, sheer determination, and a charismatic playing style that captivated fans and players alike.

Favre's journey began in Gulfport, Mississippi, where he was born on October 10, 1969. He later played college football at the University of Southern Mississippi. Despite initially being overlooked by bigger college programs, Favre made his mark at Southern Mississippi. His time in college was characterized by his gritty play and ability to produce remarkable comebacks, traits that would become hallmarks of his NFL career. His fearless playing style and strong arm caught the attention of NFL scouts, despite concerns about his rawness and decision-making.

Favre was selected by the Atlanta Falcons in the second round of the 1991 NFL Draft. However, his time with the Falcons was brief and uneventful, as he struggled to find playing time. The turning point in Favre's career came when he was traded to the Green Bay Packers in 1992. This move would prove to be pivotal, not just for Favre, but for the Packers franchise as a whole.

Once with the Packers, Favre's career trajectory changed dramatically. Thrust into the starting role early in his tenure, Favre quickly began to showcase his exceptional abilities. His arm strength, durability, and instinctive style of play made him stand out. Favre's willingness to take risks, sometimes resulting in spectacular plays and other times in costly interceptions, became a defining aspect of his game.

Favre's rise to fame was marked by a series of remarkable seasons with the Packers. He led the team to multiple playoff appearances and was instrumental in revitalizing a storied franchise that had experienced years of mediocrity. Favre's fearless approach, combined with his leadership and ability to perform in clutch situations, endeared him to fans and earned him respect across the league.

One of the most significant milestones in Favre's career was leading the Packers to victory in Super Bowl XXXI. This achievement not only cemented his status as an elite quarterback but also marked the resurgence of the Packers as a powerhouse in the NFL.

Resilience and Grit

Brett Favre's resilience and grit are epitomized by his record for consecutive starts, a remarkable feat that underscores his toughness and commitment to the game. Favre's streak of starting in 297 regular season games (321 including playoffs), spanning from 1992 to 2010, stands as a testament to his physical and mental durability.

Favre's streak of consecutive starts is not just a number; it's a narrative of playing through numerous injuries and personal tragedies, reflecting his extraordinary resilience. Over the years, he sustained various injuries that would have sidelined most players, including thumb sprains, ankle sprains, a separated shoulder, and even a broken thumb. Despite these ailments, Favre remained undeterred, often delivering some of his best performances under physical duress.

His ability to play through pain was not just about physical toughness; it also spoke to his mental grit. Favre's commitment to his team and the game was unwavering, as he consistently put the team's success ahead of his physical discomfort. This relentless drive was a source of inspiration for his teammates and a demonstration of his leadership.

Moreover, Favre's resilience was also evident in how he dealt with personal tragedies while maintaining his high level of play. One of the most poignant examples was his performance in a game against the Oakland Raiders in 2003, a day after his father, Irvin Favre, passed away. In an emotionally charged game, Favre threw for 399 yards and four touchdowns in a performance that is remembered as one of the most courageous and poignant in NFL history.

Favre's ability to maintain his consecutive starts streak also required a rigorous and disciplined approach to physical conditioning and recovery. He was proactive in his approach to injury treatment and rehabilitation, ensuring that he remained in the best possible shape to continue his streak.

Signature Playing Style

Brett Favre's signature playing style, characterized by an aggressive, risk-taking approach, made him one of the most exciting and dynamic quarterbacks in NFL history. His style of play was marked by a unique combination of raw arm strength, improvisational ability, and a willingness to take chances that few quarterbacks would dare.

Favre's arm strength was legendary. He could make throws that few others could, firing the ball downfield

with remarkable velocity and accuracy. This ability allowed him to attempt and complete passes in situations where other quarterbacks might not have even tried. Favre's fearless approach to throwing deep and into tight coverage became a defining feature of his game, thrilling fans and often catching defenses off guard.

His risk-taking style was both a strength and a vulnerability. Favre was known for attempting difficult throws, leading to spectacular plays but also resulting in a high number of interceptions. This gunslinger mentality – the willingness to take chances in pursuit of big plays – made every game unpredictable and exhilarating. While his aggressive style sometimes led to mistakes, it also resulted in some of the most memorable moments in football.

One such moment was the 1996 NFC Championship Game against the Carolina Panthers, where Favre's aggressive play was on full display. He threw for two touchdowns and 292 yards, leading the Packers to a victory and securing their place in Super Bowl XXXI. His performance in that game encapsulated his ability to make game-changing plays.

Another memorable moment was in a Monday Night Football game against the Oakland Raiders in 2003. Playing just one day after his father's death, Favre threw for 399 yards and four touchdowns in an emotionally charged performance that is widely regarded as one of the greatest in NFL history. This game showcased not just his physical skills but also his emotional resilience and leadership.

Favre's improvisational skills were also a key aspect of his playing style. He had a knack for making plays out of broken situations, often turning potential sacks or losses into big gains. His ability to extend plays with his feet and make off-balance throws added an unpredictable element to his game that was both thrilling and effective.

Challenges and Controversies

One of the major challenges Favre faced on the field was his propensity for interceptions. His aggressive, risk-taking playing style, while often leading to spectacular plays, also resulted in a high number of turnovers. Favre holds the NFL record for most career interceptions, a testament to both his longevity and his high-risk approach to the game. This aspect of his play was often a point of criticism and a challenge he had to continually address throughout his career.

Off the field, Favre faced several controversies. One of the most significant was in 2010, involving allegations of sending inappropriate messages and photos to a Jets game-day hostess while he was with the New York Jets. The scandal garnered widespread media attention and led to an NFL investigation, which resulted in Favre being fined for failing to cooperate with the investigation. This incident marred Favre's reputation and became a talking point in discussions about his legacy.

Another challenge for Favre was his series of retirements and comebacks. Towards the end of his career, he announced his retirement multiple times, only to return to play again. These indecisions, particularly around his time with the Packers and later with the Jets and Minnesota Vikings, led to media scrutiny and some criticism from fans and analysts. His wavering on retirement decisions created uncertainty and controversy both for him and the teams involved.

Favre also dealt with personal challenges, including struggles with addiction. Early in his career, he developed an addiction to painkillers, which he publicly acknowledged and sought treatment for in the mid-1990s. This battle with addiction showed a vulnerable side to Favre and highlighted the pressures and challenges faced by professional athletes.

Additionally, Favre's long career in the NFL was not without its physical toll. He endured numerous injuries, some of which were severe. His ability to play through pain and maintain his consecutive starts streak was as much a testament to his toughness as it was a source of concern for his long-term health.

Retirement and Legacy

Brett Favre's retirement and unretirement saga, along with his overall legacy in the NFL, paint a picture of a legendary player whose career was marked by both remarkable achievements and unique challenges. Favre's journey through the final years of his career and his ultimate retirement left an indelible mark on the NFL landscape.

Favre first announced his retirement from the NFL in March 2008, after 16 seasons with the Green Bay Packers. This announcement was met with a wave of tributes, reflecting his status as one of the greatest quarterbacks in the history of the league. However, this retirement was short-lived, as Favre returned to the NFL just a few months later, creating a significant stir in the sports world. He joined the New York Jets for the 2008 season, adding another chapter to his storied career.

After a single season with the Jets, Favre again announced his retirement, only to make another comeback with the Minnesota Vikings in 2009. His tenure with the Vikings was marked by some high-level performances, including leading the team to the NFC Championship Game. Favre's ability to perform at an elite level, even after multiple retirements, was a testament to his enduring skill and passion for the game.

Favre's final retirement came in 2010, after a 20-year career in the NFL. This marked the end of a journey that was as tumultuous as it was illustrious. Despite the controversies and challenges, Favre's retirement was met with widespread recognition of his contributions to the sport.

Favre's overall legacy in the NFL is significant. He left the game as one of its most prolific passers, holding numerous records at the time of his retirement, including the most career passing yards, most career touchdown passes, and most career pass completions. His record for consecutive starts, 297 regular season games (321 including playoffs), is a remarkable feat that exemplifies his durability and toughness.

Beyond the statistics, Favre's legacy is also defined by his playing style and persona. His gunslinger mentality, willingness to take risks, and ability to make extraordinary plays under pressure made him a fan favorite and a respected figure among his peers. Favre's passion for the game, evident in his energetic and enthusiastic playing style, endeared him to fans and brought a unique excitement to the sport.

Inspiring Perseverance

Brett Favre's career provides a powerful narrative on inspiring perseverance, offering valuable lessons on determination, facing adversity, and achieving longevity in one's endeavors. His journey in the NFL is a testament to the relentless pursuit of goals in the face of challenges, both personal and professional.

A key lesson from Favre's career is the importance of unwavering determination. Throughout his time in the NFL, Favre exhibited an extraordinary commitment to the sport he loved. This was evident in his willingness to play through injuries, personal struggles, and the constant pressure of professional sports. Favre's determination to succeed, regardless of the obstacles, highlights the importance of resilience and a strong will in achieving success.

Favre's career also teaches valuable lessons about facing adversity. His ability to bounce back from setbacks, whether they were poor performances, injuries, or personal struggles, demonstrates how challenges can be transformed into opportunities for growth. Favre's approach to adversity was not one of avoidance, but of confronting it head-on, learning from it, and emerging stronger. This mindset is crucial not just in sports, but in all areas of life where challenges are inevitable.

Another aspect of Favre's career that stands out is his longevity in a highly competitive and physically demanding sport. Achieving a two-decade-long career in the NFL, marked by consistent high-level performance, is a remarkable feat. This longevity can be attributed to Favre's meticulous approach to physical conditioning, mental preparation, and his ability to adapt his playing style over the years. Favre's career longevity serves as a reminder of the importance of taking care of oneself, continuously learning, and adapting to maintain relevance and effectiveness in any field.

Furthermore, Favre's journey underscores the importance of passion and love for what one does. His enthusiasm for football was infectious and a driving force behind his long career. This passion was a source of motivation that kept him going through the ups and downs of his career. It teaches that finding and nurturing a passion can be a powerful motivator and a key to long-term success.

The Revolutionary Tony Dungy

Early Career and Challenges

Born on October 6, 1955, in Jackson, Michigan, Dungy grew up in a family where education and character were emphasized. His early life was marked by a strong work ethic and a passion for football. Dungy played quarterback at Parkside High School in Jackson, showcasing early signs of the leadership and strategic thinking that would define his career. He then went on to play college football at the University of Minnesota, where he continued to play as a quarterback.

Despite a successful college career, Dungy faced challenges upon entering the NFL. In 1977, he joined the Pittsburgh Steelers as a free agent but was moved from quarterback to defensive back due to the prevailing biases and stereotypes about the quarterback position. Dungy's adaptability was on display as he made the transition to defense, demonstrating his versatility and football intelligence.

Dungy's playing career in the NFL included stints with the Steelers and the San Francisco 49ers. While he was not a standout player in the league, his understanding of the game and leadership qualities were evident. It was these attributes that laid the foundation for his transition to coaching.

After his playing career, Dungy embarked on a coaching journey that began in 1981, serving in various assistant coaching roles with the Steelers, Kansas City Chiefs, and Minnesota Vikings. His rise through the coaching ranks was marked by his calm demeanor, sharp defensive acumen, and ability to inspire and motivate players. Dungy quickly gained respect in coaching circles for his strategic mind and his unique approach to leadership.

Dungy's early coaching career was also a time when he faced and overcame significant challenges. As an African American coach in a league where diversity in leadership positions was limited, Dungy broke barriers and paved the way for future generations of coaches. His perseverance in the face of these challenges was not just a personal victory but a step forward in the fight for greater diversity and inclusion in the NFL.

Coaching Philosophy

Dungy's calm demeanor on the sidelines was one of his most notable traits. Unlike many of his contemporaries, he rarely displayed anger or frustration publicly. This composure under pressure created a stable and focused environment for his players, fostering a sense of confidence and clarity during games. Dungy believed that maintaining a calm presence helped his players perform at their best, as it allowed them to concentrate on the game without the added pressure of an emotionally reactive coach.

Central to Dungy's philosophy was the emphasis on character. He firmly believed that the key to success on the field was building a team of individuals who were not only talented athletes but also possessed strong moral character. Dungy often spoke about the importance of discipline, responsibility, and teamwork, and he sought players who embodied these values. He was known for his ability to inspire his players to strive for excellence both on and off the field.

Dungy's leadership style was also characterized by his emphasis on leading by example. He treated players, staff, and opponents with respect and expected the same from those around him. This approach earned him immense respect from his players and peers, as they saw him as a coach who practiced what he preached. His integrity and consistency in this regard were instrumental in building trust and loyalty among his team members.

Moreover, Dungy's coaching philosophy extended beyond the X's and O's of football. He was a mentor to many of his players, offering guidance and support in their personal lives as well. Dungy's holistic approach to coaching was about developing his players not just as athletes but as individuals. He believed that personal growth was crucial to team success.

His philosophy also included a focus on teamwork and collective success over individual achievements. Dungy emphasized the importance of each team member's role and the power of working together towards a common goal. This team-first mentality was a cornerstone of his coaching approach and was evident in the way his teams played.

Breaking Racial Barriers

Dungy's success in leading the Colts to a Super Bowl victory was a groundbreaking moment in the history of the league. For decades, African American coaches had faced significant challenges and obstacles in the NFL, often struggling to secure head coaching positions due to systemic biases and a lack of opportunities. Dungy's victory shattered a longstanding racial barrier, demonstrating unequivocally that African American coaches could achieve the highest levels of success in the sport.

The significance of Dungy's accomplishment extends to its impact on diversity and inclusion within the NFL. His victory served as a powerful symbol of progress and a beacon of hope for aspiring coaches of color. It challenged the status quo and sparked conversations about the importance of diversity in coaching and leadership positions in sports. Dungy's success helped pave the way for other African American coaches, inspiring them to pursue their coaching aspirations and proving that race should not be a barrier to achieving coaching excellence.

Moreover, Dungy's achievement in Super Bowl XLI was a source of pride and inspiration for the African American community. It represented a moment of triumph over historical racial barriers and prejudices, offering a vivid example of perseverance and excellence. Dungy's victory was not just celebrated as a sporting achievement but also as a significant step forward in the broader struggle for racial equality and representation.

Importantly, Dungy's approach to breaking racial barriers was characterized by his grace and integrity. He led by example, focusing on his coaching abilities and leadership qualities rather than allowing his race to define his career. His professionalism and dedication to the sport were key factors in his success, earning him respect from players, peers, and fans alike.

Mentorship and Impact

Dungy's mentorship style was characterized by his focus on character development and personal growth. He believed that a coach's role extended beyond teaching the technical aspects of the game; it also involved nurturing players and coaches as individuals. This approach led him to invest deeply in the personal and professional development of those he mentored, providing guidance, support, and wisdom.

For players, Dungy was more than a coach; he was a role model and a father figure. He took a keen interest in their lives outside of football, offering advice and support  in areas ranging from financial management to personal relationships. His focus on building strong character was evident in the way he encouraged players to be responsible, disciplined, and community-oriented. Many players credited Dungy with not only helping them improve their game but also with making them better people.

Dungy also played a pivotal role in mentoring other coaches, particularly African American coaches. He was instrumental in promoting diversity within the coaching ranks, using his influence to open doors and provide opportunities for minority coaches. Dungy's mentorship helped prepare the next generation of coaches, equipping them with the skills, knowledge, and values necessary to succeed in the NFL.

One of Dungy's most notable mentees is Mike Tomlin, whom Dungy hired as a defensive backs coach with the Tampa Bay Buccaneers. Tomlin, who would go on to become the head coach of the Pittsburgh Steelers and win a Super Bowl, often spoke of the profound impact Dungy had on his career and life. Dungy's mentorship of Tomlin is just one example of his broader impact on the coaching community.

Dungy's influence extended beyond the individuals he directly mentored. His leadership style and philosophy had a ripple effect throughout the NFL, inspiring other coaches and players to adopt similar approaches. His emphasis on integrity, humility, and the importance of balancing professional success with personal well-being has left a lasting mark on the sport.

Personal Life and Advocacy

Tony Dungy's personal life, marked by strong family values and advocacy for various causes, reflects the depth of his character and his commitment to making a positive impact beyond the football field. His personal endeavors provide insight into the man behind the coaching legend, revealing a life dedicated to family, faith, and community service.

Family has always been a central aspect of Dungy's life. He and his wife, Lauren, have been deeply involved in their children's lives, emphasizing the importance of family bonds and shared values. Dungy's approach to fatherhood mirrors his approach to coaching, focusing on character development, guidance, and leading by example. He has often spoken about the importance of balancing his professional responsibilities with his role as a husband

and father, striving to be present and involved in his family's life.

Dungy's faith is another cornerstone of his personal life. A devout Christian, his faith has shaped his worldview and his approach to both his professional career and personal endeavors. He has been open about the role of faith in guiding his decisions and actions, emphasizing themes of forgiveness, compassion, and service to others. Dungy's faith has been a source of strength and inspiration throughout his life, influencing his interactions and choices.

In addition to his family and faith, Dungy has been a vocal advocate for various causes. He has used his platform to promote and support community service, education, and youth development programs. Dungy has been involved in numerous charitable activities, including work with organizations focused on children and families, mentoring initiatives, and programs aimed at improving the lives of disadvantaged youth.

One of Dungy's significant advocacy roles has been his involvement in prison ministries and efforts to support formerly incarcerated individuals. He has been passionate about helping these individuals reintegrate into society and rebuild their lives, reflecting his belief in redemption and second chances.

Dungy has also been an advocate for mental health awareness, particularly in the wake of personal tragedy. After the loss of his son, James, to suicide, Dungy and his family have been open about their experiences with grief and mental health. They have worked to break down the stigma surrounding mental health issues and have encouraged open discussions about seeking help and support.

Furthermore, Dungy has been an influential voice in discussions about race, diversity, and inclusion, both within the NFL and in broader society. His experiences as an African American coach and his commitment to promoting diversity and equality have made him a respected figure in conversations about these critical issues.

Legacy Beyond the Field

Tony Dungy's legacy extends far beyond the football field, characterized by his unwavering integrity, exceptional leadership, and deep commitment to community involvement. His influence in these areas has made a lasting impact, shaping not just the world of sports but also the broader societal landscape.

Dungy's integrity has been a defining feature of his legacy. In a profession often marked by intense pressure and high stakes, Dungy consistently maintained his principles, both in his coaching career and personal life. He is widely respected for his ethical approach to coaching, prioritizing character and moral values over winning at any cost. This commitment to integrity has set a standard in the NFL and has been a guiding light for coaches, players, and fans alike.

In terms of leadership, Dungy's influence has been profound. His leadership style, characterized by calmness, respect, and positivity, has redefined what it means to be a successful leader in the high-pressure environment of professional sports. Dungy's approach to leadership, focusing on mentorship, personal development, and leading by example, has been emulated by many in and out of sports. His emphasis on the importance of being a role model has inspired countless individuals to adopt a similar approach in their leadership roles.

Dungy's community involvement has also been a significant aspect of his legacy. He has been actively involved in various charitable and community initiatives, using his platform to advocate for important causes and to make a positive difference in the lives of others. His work with children and families, educational programs, and support for formerly incarcerated individuals has had a tangible impact on communities. Dungy's commitment to community service exemplifies how individuals can use their influence to effect positive change.

Additionally, Dungy's role in promoting mental health awareness and his advocacy for diversity and inclusion have extended his impact beyond the football arena. By speaking openly about personal challenges and championing the cause of equality, Dungy has contributed to important societal conversations and initiatives. His efforts in these areas have helped to break down stigmas and promote a more inclusive and understanding society.

Dungy's legacy is also evident in the way he has inspired others to pursue their goals with integrity, humility, and a commitment to excellence. His life story and career serve as powerful examples of how perseverance, grounded in strong values, can lead to success and fulfillment.

References

Young, Jeff C. *Devin Hester*. Mason Crest Publishers (2009)

Mendiola, Jordan. *The Complete Story of Tom Brady (The GOAT)*. Medium (2022). https://medium.com/long-term-perspective/the-complete-story-of-tom-brady-36cb0c89be41. Accessed December 02, 2023

Moyer, Susan M. *Reggie White: A Celebration of Life, 1961-2004*. Sports Publishing LLC (2005)

Mullen, Robert. *The Greatest Show on Turf: The Story of 99-01 St. Louis Rams*. Outskirts Press, Incorporated (2009)

Heits, Rudolph T. *Jason Witten*. Mason Crest Publishers (2010)

Parker, John. *Vince Lombardi: Everything That Is Great About Football*. Bleacher Report (2008). https://bleacherreport.com/articles/82038-vince-lombardi-everything-that-is-great-about-football. Accessed November 29, 2023

Borelli, Stephen. *The story of Doug Williams, celebrated now, was hardly a fairy tale: He faced ugly racism*. USA TODAY (2023). https://www.usatoday.com/story/sports/nfl/super-bowl/2023/02/12/doug-williams-story-celebrated-now-hardly-fairy-tale/11238198002/. Accessed November 30, 2023

Turner, Mark Tye. *Notes from a 12 Man: A Truly Biased History of the Seattle Seahawks*. Sasquatch Books (2010)

Fantasy Boss. *New England Patriots 2016 Super Bowl LI Champion Season Statistic Logbook: All Game And Individual Statistics From The 2016 Season*. CreateSpace Independent Publishing Platform (2017)

Taylor, Roy. *Walter Payton, Bears RB, 1975-1987*. Bears History (2002). http://www.bearshistory.com/lore/walterpayton.aspx. Accessed Dec 03, 2023

Willard, Samuel. *Peyton Manning*. Chelsea House (2015).

Dulac, Gerry. *Catch of a lifetime: Legendary 'Immaculate Reception' lives on 50 years later*. Pro Football Hall of Fame (2023). https://www.profootballhof.com/news/2022/catch-of-a-lifetime-legendary-immaculate-reception-lives-on-50-years-later/. Accessed December 04, 2023

Bishop, Chad. *A First for Fuller ... and for All*. Vu Commodores (2020). https://vucommodores.com/a-first-for-fuller-and-for-all/. Accessed November 28, 2023

Gruver, Ed. *The Ice Bowl: The Cold Truth About Football's Most Unforgettable Game*. Lyons Press (2021)

Bordow, Scott. *Cardinals fullback Derrick Coleman is deaf and was bullied as a kid; now he has a Super Bowl ring*. The Athletic (2018). https://theathletic.com/680028/2018/11/28/

cardinals-fullback-derrick-coleman-is-deaf-and-was-bullied-as-a-kid-now-he-has-a-super-bowl-ring/. Accessed November 30, 2023

Beard, Alison. *Life's Work: An Interview with Jerry Rice*. Harvard Business Review (2022). https://hbr.org/2022/09/lifes-work-an-interview-with-jerry-rice. Accessed December 05, 2023

Koestler-Grack, Rachel A. *Brett Favre*. Chelsea House Publisher (2015).

Fischer, Ben. *Tony Dungy: The Conscience of the NFL*. Sports Business Journal (2021). https://www.sportsbusinessjournal.com/Journal/Issues/2021/09/20/Champions/Dungy.aspx. Accessed December 01, 2023

Bonus: Free Book!

Are you ready to delve into the *Inspiring Soccer Stories* for free? Get ready to go deep into the world soccer? Just use your smartphone or tablet to scan the QR code below, then follow the simple prompts to receive the PDF.

www.ingramcontent.com/pod-product-compliance
Lightning Source LLC
Chambersburg PA
CBHW052101110526
44591CB00013B/2309